Lemons

A poetry collection

s a w h n e y

ISBN 978-1-54396-183-6 (print)
ISBN: 978-1-54396-184-3 (ebook)
Library of Congress Control Number

1st Edition, 2019
Printed in the United States of America

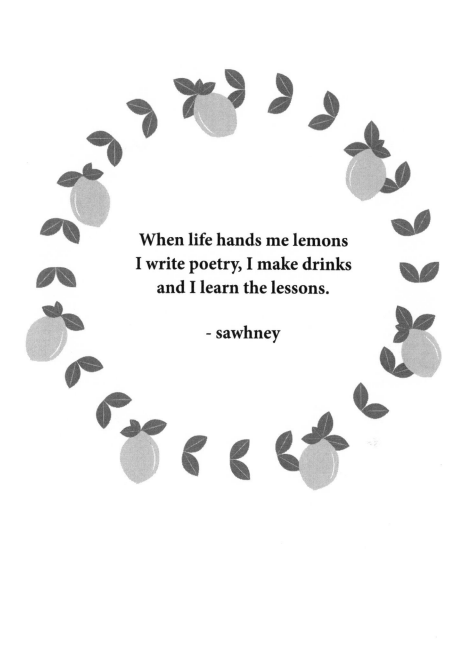

When life hands me lemons
I write poetry, I make drinks
and I learn the lessons.

- sawhney

LEMONS

Sometimes life hands me lemons
Other days
I walk through my garden
Up to a big, bright, succulent lemon tree
And I pluck
The ripest fruits
Hanging heavy from the weight of fertility

I go inside
And cut them up
Squeeze out the juice
Add sugar
A pinch of salt
Water
And I suck
On the glorious juice
My labors produced

After a smooth gulp
I set my glass down

I'm unsatisfied.

I did this
Knowing all along
I was just quenching the wrong thirst
When
All I wanted
Was to take big happy gulps
From the fresh

Cool
Ever flowing
Water hose
Lying alongside
The garden's dirt road

I walked straight past the
Coiled
Green
Fountain of youth
Because I thought I wanted
What the others said was good

Lemons may look like gold
But I knew
That the crystalline-clear diamond waters
That ran amongst the heavenly brown earth
Always quenched my thirst

Some days life hands me lemons
Other days I pick the damn fruit myself

Move Around

Move, move
Don't let your body
Become your thoughts' fool

Stir yourself.
Bring movement to life.
Your thoughts are nothing but time spent
If you don't move around.

Natural Peace

When you walk
Through my garden
Do you find what you're looking for?
Have you taken the time
To smell the roses?
Do you get close to the ground
To see more?

What do you see?
Do you like the way the lilies
Call out to you?
Have you found your way
Across the dandelions
And through the redwood trees?

Will you pluck what you see
Or will you love the flowers enough
To let them grow and let them be?

When you walk through the garden
I hope you find what you're looking for
I hope you find my natural peace

Muse (Take 1)

Will you be my muse
Will you be the one

I spend countless hours on
Writing out my thoughts
With the perfect imperfections
You possess?

Will you be the one
Whose being inspires me?
The one
Whose smile will bring countless joys to me?
Will you be
My lover and friend?
Will you inspire generations
As you conspire with my pen?
Will you be the gateway
To my art?
My soul? My heaven?
Will you live past forever?
On and on to forever and a half?

Will you inspire my heart?
I really must know
Will you -
Will you be
The muse
For my art?

Caressing Flowered Hearts

He says he likes my flower garden
He's seen it through a glass window
And despite the distance
He uses the distorted vision to admire
My beauty from afar

He admires my luscious garden
And hopes that up close and personal
The wildflowers are nothing less than sweet

He wants to walk through my garden
He wants to see what I've got
He wants to breathe in the rose hips
He wants to caress flowered hearts

But when he encounters the Garden of Eden
What will he do?
Will he pluck the flowers?
Or will he toss fruitful seeds
And then water the lot?

Diamond in the Rough

I'm a diamond
I'm a diamond in the rough
You want to touch me
You want to hold me
You want me to be yours
You want to be mine
But you don't
Don't want to get dirty
Don't want to be covered in the mud
Yet you want me
You want the diamond in the rough

You're out there searching
Searching for perfection
Perfection because
You think you deserve it
But you don't
Don't listen to the advice from friends and family
So you keep looking up high
Cause you don't
Don't want to be covered in mud
So you keep passing me by
Afraid to get dirty
Passing the diamond in the rough

I can't change your eyes
I can't change your vision
Or your approach
I'm just a diamond
Who you are not ready to uncover from this earth

You need to come down to ground level
Enjoy the dirt and the mud
Love the richness around you
Love your world
Before you're ready
For this diamond in the rough

Please keep searching
Please keep yearning for what it is you think you deserve
Never stop hoping
Never stop searching
For your diamond in the rough

One day you'll find your gem
The precious diamond in the mud
And you'll understand
This gem wasn't made for you
To have and to hold and to keep to yourself

This gem was made
To be adored and loved
In her natural element
Lovingly surrounded by the earth and the mud

One day,
You'll find a diamond
That precious diamond in the rough
And if you do get dirty
Just remember one thing

You can always wash off the mud.

Your Storm

When I looked toward you
I saw a storm forming in your eyes
a mix of emotions clashing before mine
I saw despair
and I saw hope
and I wondered
Why did the world bring us together
once more?

Did I see hope
because, perhaps,
you never stopped loving me?
Or did I see despair
because
in this moment
you're now all alone?

The storm is just starting.

Moving Forward

Moving forward
forever still
sights ahead
heart beating grows
mouth slightly parched
breath forgotten
and still

Moving forward

Away I must go
off to see another world
off to explore
Where am I going?
you've yet to see
Where will I end?
the answer is forever changing

Moving forward
lost in half of my senses
aroused by my ideas
troubled by my thoughts
I'll go there
and I'll go ahead
never backwards

I'll go forward
I'll go everywhere

Out to the realms
underneath a cover of stars
shaded by a layer of sun
drenched in the shades
of loud emotions
that soak me
throughout the end of the days
and the start of nights

I've given myself
to you,
dear world,
I give myself
to you

Moving forward
surrounded by your shades of darkness and light
I give myself to you

Forever still,
Moving forward

Bitter/Sweet

I say to myself
"Shh, shh,
Be quiet. You said you were done doing this
- dreaming -
You said you were going to live in reality."

But when I take a bite of reality
The bitter juice stings
As it drips down my lips
Then I feel the acrid taste
Overtaking my mouth

The taste starts to take me over
Slowly staining my senses
My eyes,
My ears,
My touch, my heart

Then, the bitter becomes me

I don't want this
I don't want to be something I am not
I don't want to leave a bitter mark
Wherever I go, on whatever I touch

I want to be free
I want to be sweet

I want to pollinate
The fields around me

With my sweetness
Like a precious honey bee
That only gives its best
To the world around it
Giving a little
To create
Beautiful fields of smiling flowers
Enhancing aromas that make the senses come alive
Producing sounds that bring your attention to this varied life

I want to give goodness
That is who I want to be

But before that happens
Maybe I'll need to know bitter
To know how to be sweet

And maybe I'll need to know another reality
To learn how to cultivate my dreams

Seasons of Your Love

I hope you relentlessly love me
Accept my all
Explore with me and be my partner
Through the sun and snowfall

Hold me tight through the winter
Warm me up
Show me the seasons of your deep love

And before you know it
The summer's heat
Will inspire us
To love deep
And to love hard

Love me from winter to summer
Then from summer to winter
Over and over
Harder and deeper
So the seasons don't outlast our love

I want to grow this love
Past forever
After the rains stop
After the moon falls

I want to know all the seasons that make up your love

Sing to me, Sunshine

Sing to me, sunshine
Take my pains away
Tell me your dreams
Tell me your fears
Shine on the darkness
And take away the grey

Curves & Hollow Spaces

The forces are pulling me
In opposite directions
One forcing me to stay
Like an anchor at the foot of a boat in a shallow harbor
Docked and waiting
For something out of the ordinary to happen

The tide rises and falls,
But these are small changes for a boat
That's crossed deep curves and floated atop hollow spaces

Even with the anchor pulled up
The vessel won't go very far in these waters

Meanwhile, the sea breezes and trade winds pull me
They ask me to come their way
To find mysteries and risks
To swim the curves and deep hollows I've only known in
my Dreams
Whatever dangers I may encounter
I hope they will be worth the pain of living life freely
And perhaps the life I discover will only treat me dearly...

What more could I ask for
Than to look face to face with life upon the glorious sea?

The truth doesn't need to be told
It needs to be lived
And breathed, and feared, and loved.
But,
When the safe waters and the anchor call,

I hope I choose the life I've always dreamed of
The anchor can hold me steady if the time is right,
But the time is now!

I've got to see the life
Amidst the deep waters
Amongst the curves and hollow spaces
I must experience a life
Made for me:
free.

Raindrops

Raindrops
They fell.

Tear drops
They dripped and dropped and dried.

The agonies
They passed.

The heartache
I survived.

When the waters came
I found a place for cover.

When the pain arrived
I learned to take refuge
In myself.

The rain stopped; yet
The clouds covered the skies
Tricking us into believing
More rain would come.

The pain subsided
And persisted
I tried to heal myself
I questioned the paths I would take.

When the sun started
To come through the clouds
I hesitated to looked out.

I did not want to be too eager
To see the clouds part.

I was scared to be let down
By the clouds who could open for the moment
And continue to let the rain come down.

I saw the light continue
I allowed myself
To find comfort
In the blossoming sky.

I witnessed the sun drying the ground
Feeding the plants and earth.

I found myself drying my tears
Finding new places and people
Stories and adventures
Feeding the soul.

I saw the world come alive
I found peace in my pain.

I found peace.
I found a reason for the pain.

Muse (Take 2)

I hope I will find you
So I can spend
My time
Writing out
My thoughts on
The perfect imperfections
You wholeheartedly possess

I hope you are the one
Who inspires me
The one
Whose radiant smile
Brings countless joys to life

You are mine
My lover and friend
You were made
To inspire generations
As you conspire
With my pen
Thank you
For being you,
A gateway for my art

You've added to my life
Brought richness to my soul
And I hope you live on
Past forever and a half
When you inspire my heart

Here I am
Wanting so much
Wanting to give you my world

I really must know
Will you be
The muse
For my art?

Driving through the Andes, 2017

Neil Young
Blasting on the radio
Windows down
The fresh mountain air hits us fast
While we cruise through the middle of everywhere

Off in the distance
And all around
The Andes rise up
Blessing us in the presence
Of their snow-capped crowns

I want to remember this moment
Past forever and a half
This moment is perfect
The perfect place to find
When I want to run away and forget

This is the perfect memory to uncover
When I am
Stuck between here
And there
This
And that
Stuck in a day
I am forced
To have

When I feel trapped
On a cold winter day

After three alarm snoozes
And the walls close in
On my warm body and stiff neck
I take myself back
To the day spent
Embracing the mountains
The day spent
Feeling free
And light
As the fresh mountain air hits us
And the radio blasts

Can you come look at the stars with me?

Can you come look at the stars with me?
I just want it to be you and me
Get ready and I'll be there in 10
We will drive up the mountain
A quick getaway
Bring hot chocolate, a blunt, and a blanket
Using this time to take our minds away from all of our yesterdays

Let's gaze at the sky
Like star-crossed lovers and friends
On our quiet escape to the end of outer space

Just you and me and the stars
The perfect Saturday night
Light up the blunt
Take in the smoke
Lace it with fresh mountain air
Exhale our daily sorrows
Our doubts, our fears
And our "I don't cares"
Letting go of yesterday and today and tomorrow
Just you and me and the stars
Enjoying this perfect moment
Like there's no yesterday, tomorrow, today

We sit still
And we watch
We stare with unending delight
Pull the blanket close to us
Breathe deep and steady

As we consider our faults
Under the lights in the skies
We talk about the "what ifs"
The "I think I can do it's"
And the hopes of all our tomorrows
While reality starts to set in
Our necks begin to ache
As we look up at the stars
We take one final breath to remind us
That these are our forevers
Our yesterdays
Our tomorrows
And our todays

Young & Reckless

The young and the reckless
Who are you?
You disappear on wild rides
To the gates of heaven
Only coming back to earth
To resurrect your youth

What is your fuel?
Is it anger
Or money?
Why do we do this
While riding spaceships
To the dark side of the moon?

Love is expensive
So is time
Cigarettes and white packs fuel the fire:
Money is a pastime

Wild and free,
At least that's what I claim to be

Trapped by demons
Who set my soul on fire
Reckless youth
Burning the fire in me

Every Other Season

I come and I'm gone
Every other season
If you really loved me
You'd know I can't sit still;
I move around
That's my living reason.

So don't tell me you love me
And we're meant to be
Because you failed to recognize
This honest reality

You don't love the movement
That became me
You're just in love
With the idea of who I almost was

I am not the woman you want me to be

2 Second Lesson

"What do you want from me?"
I whisper to him slowly
I can't speak any louder because I'm scared to speak,
Scared to hear his reply

He stares back in silence
Not moving a muscle
But his eyes tell me
His mind is formulating an answer

So I wait
2 seconds too long for someone who always has
Something to say.
That's when I know
He doesn't know what he wants.

He just wanted my time, my presence...
Until he figured it out.
Until he knew exactly what he wanted
He wanted me slowly
To fill him
With my love
To please
His unfulfilled soul
The way he loved the others

So after his 2 second pause
I step back,
Speaking with my body
What my silent words are unable to formulate

He moves forward
But not enough
A half-hearted, defeated sigh quickly escapes
As his mouth opens then closes up
Knowing he's lost this battle
Knowing I
May be gone for good

He had his opportunity
And away it went
So I cross my arms
Turn my face to the other side
And slowly move back
Signaling to him my goodbye.

"I thought so," I say. My words sting as they leave my mouth.
"But, no, it's just..." He tries to reply.
But I'm already moving forward,
Ready to go on
I take a great leap forward tonight
And continue ahead tomorrow
My body has been waiting to move on.

As always,
I give him a piece of my heart.
Perhaps this is my last attempt to be a friend
"If you want to talk about this later, fine.
But don't act as if you want more when you don't know.
I gotta go.
I'll see you later...
Bye."

Those were my last words
I grab my keys from my bag

And walk to my car
Knowing he's shocked
Knowing I've done
What I've been needing to do
For far too long

It feels good to stand up for myself, I decide as I walk alone.
But I'm not so good at goodbyes
And it's hard when I need to say bye to a friend
And part-time lover
Possibly forever...
For now, this is how it will end.

Goodbye false lover,
You don't deserve me
Cause you didn't want me to the end

I'm glad I loved you for a small while
But it seems you forgot -
I know too much.
Did you forget the hours we spent speaking our hearts
To one another,
Sharing our stories of loves found and lost?
Or reliving the moments of perfection
We encountered
Amidst life's chaos?
You knew me before the lust,
You knew me when we were young and curiously dumb

I wanted what you always gave
Friendship and Hope.
But now,
It seems that you don't know what you want from me.

And I don't know you anymore.
Goodbye.

Modern Day Mona Lisa

I'm an accidental masterpiece
You wished you had me
After you noticed
I was gone
Way back when
You overlooked me
Looked forward
Looked back
And
Poof!
Your senses were lost

When you try to find me now
You can see
But you'll never touch

Can you see her? Can you see the hidden meaning behind the art?
When they ask you what you see
When you describe the art you lost
You tell them,
Full of lustful regret,
She looks something like a modern day Mona Lisa

I'm the masterpiece you once lost
The one you'll never forget

Home, Sweet, Home

Where is home?
They say it is where your heart lies.

But,
Oh,
My heart is everywhere and nowhere.
I am lost.

Temptation's Eyes

When I look temptation in the eyes
I see his seductive smile
I hear the empty promises
That make my legs tight
I feel the ravenous look
Fleeing from his eyes

And I come close

Close enough to feel his breath
Heavy and excited to breathe a new life into me
Close enough to feel his beating heart,
The rhythm that his hips will later follow
Close enough to make one small move
That takes me past
The point of no return

I could give in,
I could give in to the temptation
That swallows me up
That will bring a momentary passion
To my body
This is a fast burning, youthful fuel
Hot and fiery, temptation could take me if I let him

What if
It could be something
Else?
Something
More?

But I have known enough of these passionate moments
To know
This is all it is, all it could be

And in the back of my mind
Something stronger
Than the touch of a man
Ignites me

I feel
The hope and peace
That is you

I crave your slow burning, steady fire.
I remind myself
That you have given me
A hope for something better
Something more
Something
That will burn
Forever

If I allow it

I take a deep breath, straighten my body
And I look temptation in the eyes
Then I tell him
To move along

I was made to love you.

Magic of the Mind

I believe in the magic
Of my mind
And the light of the stars
Guiding me
Through the night

I believe there is more
Than living a scared life
So I tell myself to envision
The life I was meant to live

When I see the miracles
Of everyday life
Who am I to say
That those miracles
Are not enough to convince me
To continue searching
For something more than good
And greater than great

I push aside the doubts
I celebrate the beauty
The small miracles bring to life
And I look toward the
Positive direction
The blessings have laid out for me

I see something more
For me
I hope you see something better for you

The Night Sky

The night sky
is my dear mother
she shines bright
with hope
always giving me the necessary signals
never sending the messages
too close

The night sky
is my angel
protective and loving
here to watch
never to control

She sends me signals
and then
I make my choice

She loves what she sees
I love
what she has to offer

The night sky
is my protector

She loves me
She shields me
She was made
to show me
what it means to be

both free and full of life

She is my savior
She is the night

Runaway

Too much lust
No room for love
Too much hate
Where's my heart
You ran away from me
Only coming back
When you have needs
You ran away
You only come back
When you lose sight of me

When you leave me alone
I find my peace
My eyes wander
To see the prospects I can reap

But wandering eyes
Don't find the truth
They make space
For alternate realities

I found myself gone
While I was looking up
At the dreams in the sky
And then I loved what I lost
When I lost focus on you

World Watching

I could watch the world forever
I could watch life living
her exciting life

I observe the world with unending delight

I become overjoyed
watching the clouds pass me by
as the seasons come
and pass
I watch the cold and the rainy,
the wickedly icy
the pleasant thaw
then the wonderfully delicious
summer heat
and back to the cold
with its friend,
the rain

I observe the cars driving on the freeway

I see the cars drive past
one after another
each box
carrying its own lives
on their journey
to another place,
another time

I take myself
to another world
to another realm
another lovely place
to watch life

I see the lights
of a city wrapped in gold
that fill me up
with energy radiating from other lives
out into the unknown

When the night has dawned
and the skies
speak loud whispers
while the earth-dwellers
dream on
I find myself lost
under a sea in the sky
the most wonderful mystery
of them all

Under her guidance and company
the night sky
takes my hand
showing me
a world of magical diamonds
an ethereal masterpiece
I've never touched
but have always hungered to know

Take me away
and wrap me in your magic

Show me a world
I was made
to see
Show me a world
that comes to life
amidst the unknown

If I could, I would free myself
into all the other worlds

I could spend this life
watching the cars pass by
I could watch the universe live its life

Simplicity

I need simplicity in my life
Just a quiet night
Mind wrapped up
In a book
Body wrapped up
In a blanket
And nothing more
To distract me
From what could be
Or what was not

I find that time
Is betraying me
And my mind
Is tagging along for fun
Because I've got little else to do
I've got little else
To focus on

I need simplicity in my life
A warm mug
A steeping tea bag
A little cream
One teaspoon of brown, brown sugar
And nothing more
Than the deep breaths of my lungs
The pumping of my heart
I want nothing more
Than an evening spent
In the peaceful madness

Of my mind

I want to be away
From it all
But running away
Never helped

I just delay the pain and the gratitude
The further I run away

If no peace today
I'll search for the simple happiness tonight

Let us be simple
Away from the madness
Of a
Chaotic
And an
Unending
And a
Messy
Life

Alone
In simplicity
Alone
Simply breathing in
What is and what could be
And exhaling
Life

Lemons